For Teresa

The Standard Publishing Company, Cincinnati, Ohio
A division of Standex International Corporation
© 1994 by The Standard Publishing Company
All rights reserved.
Printed in the United States of America
01 00 99 97 96 95 94   5 4 3 2 1

Library of Congress Catalog Card Number 94-1127
ISBN 0-7847-0199-7
Cataloging-in-Publication data available
Edited by Diane Stortz   Designed by Coleen Davis

LITTLE DEER
B·O·O·K·S
PSALM 42:1

Standard Publishing
Cincinnati, Ohio

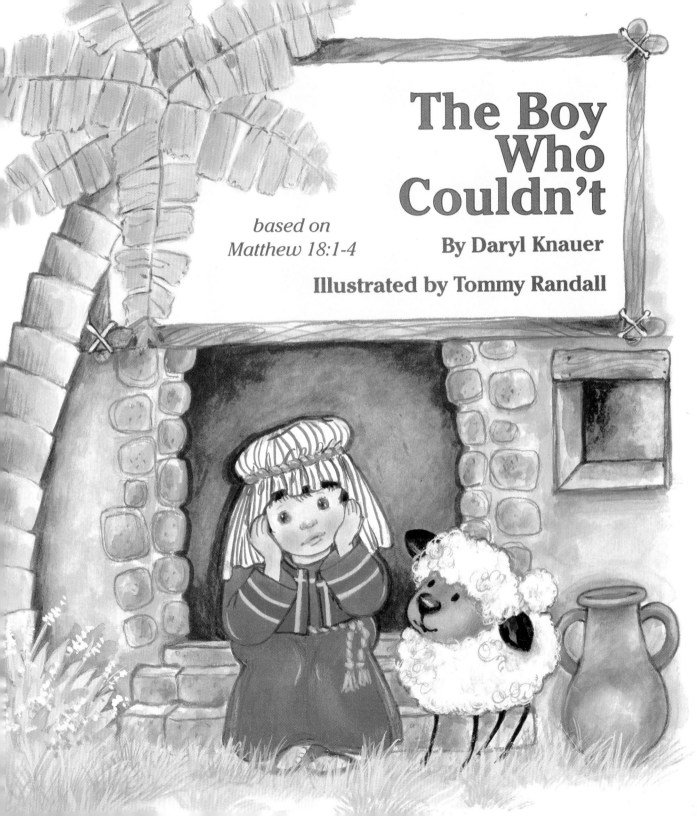

The Boy Who Couldn't

based on
Matthew 18:1-4

By Daryl Knauer

Illustrated by Tommy Randall

"I tell you the truth,
unless you change
and become like little children,
you will never enter
the kingdom of God."
Matthew 18:3

Everyone in Benjamin's family was older than Benjamin. Everyone could do things that Benjamin couldn't do.

"I wish I was older," said Benjamin. "You're growing every day!" said Grandfather. "Just you wait." Benjamin couldn't wait to grow up.

Benjamin walked
to the village square
with Mother. The older boys
were choosing sides
for tug-of-war.
No one chose Benjamin.
"You are too little,"
the older boys said.

The younger children were running races.
Benjamin ran fast.
His leather sandals slapped loudly
against his feet.
But Benjamin did not win the race.
His feet couldn't carry him fast enough.

Benjamin went home.
His brother, Caleb, was reading his lessons.
"Can I read, too?" asked Benjamin.
"You are too young," said Caleb.
"But you can try."

Benjamin held the scroll
like Caleb did.
But he couldn't read the words.

Next Benjamin walked to the orchard
where Father was picking figs.
Benjamin tried to pluck ripe figs
from the branches.
But his arms couldn't reach the fruit.

"When you are older," said Father,
"you will be able to help."
Father gave Benjamin
a handful of figs
to put in a basket.
But Benjamin's stomach couldn't wait.

When Benjamin had eaten
his fill of sweet figs, he ran to the shore
to watch the fishing boats with Grandfather.
"Go away. We're busy working here,"
said a man mending a net.
"This is no place for children."

"It is all right," Grandfather said.
"The boy is with me."
Benjamin stood in the cool water
and squished mud between his toes.

A fishing boat was dragging a net
full of fish to the shore.
"I will help you,"
Benjamin called to the fishermen.
The men on the boat laughed.
"Come back when you are older,
small fry.
Then we will teach you to fish."

"I will help *now*," said Benjamin.
He pulled and tugged,
but he couldn't lift the heavy net.

On his way home, Benjamin ran back through town.
In the square was a man he had seen before.
The man's name was Jesus.
Grandfather said Jesus was the wisest person he knew.
A group of men were sitting around Jesus,
and they were talking all at once.

Benjamin stopped to listen.
"Tell us, Jesus," said the men.
"Who is the greatest
in the kingdom of heaven?"

Benjamin was sure
he knew the answer.
*The greatest is someone
who is fast and smart
and tall and strong,*
he thought.

Jesus held his arms
out to Benjamin.
"Come stand beside me,"
Jesus said.
Benjamin's eyes got big.
What does Jesus want?
he wondered.
I'm being good.

He stood next to Jesus.
"I'm telling you
the truth," said Jesus.
"Whoever humbles
himself
like this child
is the greatest
in the kingdom
of heaven."

Like me? thought Benjamin.
I can't run fast. I can't read. I'm not tall.
I can't catch fish. But Jesus says a child
like me is the greatest in the kingdom of heaven!

Benjamin couldn't believe his ears.

"I guess I *can* wait to grow up!"
shouted Benjamin as he ran
all the way home.
"Because Jesus says it's *good*
to be a child like me!"

Benjamin couldn't wait
to tell his family!

Heart-to-Heart

A child snuggled on your lap, a book in hand—what an opportunity to explore your child's inner world!

Your child's reactions to a story are an open window into her thoughts and feelings. So ask questions. Probe for ideas and feelings. Ask your child what he would do if he were one of the characters. Let him suggest other endings to the story.

Not only will you be talking to your child, heart-to-heart—you'll also make every story you read uniquely your own. Here are some questions you might weave into this book the next time you read it to your child.

• Benjamin liked to run races and eat figs. What games do you like to play? What foods do you like to eat?

• Tell me what others in your family can do that you can't do. Would you like to be able to do those things? Why?

• Tell me what you can do that others in your family *can't* do.

• God made each of us different. We like to do different things. Tell me about something you like to do that makes you happy.

• If you were Benjamin, how would you feel when you stood near Jesus? What do you think you might have said to Jesus?

•What do you like about being a child? What don't you like?

RACING on the WATER

by John Feilen

Library of Congress Catalog Card Number: 76-5638.
International Standard Book Number: 0-913940-40-2.

Revised 1977

Design— Doris Woods, Randal M. Heise

Two-time world champion "Pay 'N Pak" is an unlimited hydroplane, fastest kind of racing boat.

RACING on the WATER

Large racing yachts, such as this beautiful schooner, are becoming very rare.

There's no telling when the first boat race took place.

Maybe two cave-men raced rafts on a foaming river. Or they might have matched speeds in skin-covered, wood-frame coracles, or even in hollowed-out logs. But there's one thing you can be sure of — just as soon as human beings invented boats, they must have thought about racing them!

Indians raced canoes. Eskimoes raced kayaks. Vikings raced dragon-prowed longboats. Romans raced their galleys. Boats are a useful form of transport, but they have also appealed to human sporting instincts.

Racing on the water — in any kind of craft that floats — is an ancient pastime that is just as much fun today as it was in the Stone Age. However, today's water racer is luckier than the cave-man. Modern racers have all kinds of boats to choose from. And new ones are being invented every day.

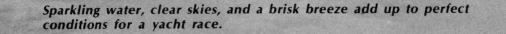

The most famous boat race of all is the America's Cup yacht race. It started in 1851 when the New York Yacht Club challenged England's Royal Yacht Squadron to race.

The Yankee boat, a schooner named America, took on 17 assorted British yachts as Queen Victoria watched. America whipped the entire crowd with ridiculous ease. The second-place yacht trailed two miles astern.

America brought home a silver trophy as a

symbol of victory. It became known as the America's Cup.

For the next 123 years, yachts from England, Canada, Ireland, Australia, France and elsewhere challenged the United States to defend America's Cup. There have been 22 competitions since 1951, the last in 1974.

American yachts have won all of them. The 1974 contest was won by the 12-meter Courageous, which beat the Southern Cross of Australia 4 races to 0.

Today, racing sailboats are divided into three big classes — Ocean Racers, Keel Boats, and Small Class Boats.

Small boats, such as this dinghy, have the most appeal of all. They are not terribly expensive to buy or to operate, and they require crews of only one or two people.

The most dedicated dinghy racers choose high-performance craft such as the Finn (which has a class in the yachting event of the Olympic Games).

People who are not expert sailors, or those who want a boat that is good for cruising as well as racing, choose less-sensitive dinghies. It is possible to race even family dinghies. Or you can compromise on a boat such as the 505, shown in this picture. It is an exciting racing craft, but also offers safe cruising.

The 505's racing in the picture have set their spinnakers. This is an extra sail, usually made of bright-colored cloth, that helps a racing yacht to achieve greater speed.

Small boat races take place on rivers, ponds, lakes, and sheltered sea inlets. Thousands of these contests are held every year. Even very young children can take part in dinghy races.

The most intense competition in yacht racing comes in the Ocean Racing class. Among the most famous races for these larger boats are the Newport (R.I.) to Bermuda Race, the Trans-Pacific Race, and the Chicago to Mackinac Island Race. The latter is raced on Lake Michigan, of course, not on the ocean. But the Great Lakes are so large and deep that they are really "inland seas" as far as yachtsmen are concerned.

Winning a yacht race calls for speed and luck. Even the best crew and the sleekest boat can be defeated by sailing into a "dead " patch of water — one with little or no breeze. The racing skipper is always observing the wind, steering, and trimming sail to get the best performance out of his boat.

If he is lucky, a good wind may send his craft whizzing along at nearly 25 miles per hour. If the wind is light, the boat may move along with maddening slowness. Or there may be a squall, with high winds that strain both boat and crew to the limit. Whatever happens, the race will end with the crew dead tired — and eager for the next race.

Two 24-footers compete on the open sea.

Fans watch a Cracker Box class Inboard racer as it tears up the water of Long Beach Marine Stadium, California. The boat has a 15-foot Patterson hull and is powered by a 262 cubic inch Ford V-8 engine. Its top speed is 90 mph.

Powerboats are even older than autos. The very first one wheezed down the River Seine in Paris in 1887. It coughed and died after traveling only a few yards. But only a few years later, boat engines became reliable — and powerboat sailors began to race.

The first trophy race for powerboats took place in 1903. The winning speedster achieved a velocity of 18 knots. Today's rooster-tailing hydroplanes go a bit faster. Say, 200 miles an hour faster!

Powerboat racing for the non-rich began in 1909 when Ole Evinrude of Wisconsin built the first practical, cheap outboard motor. His little putt-putt had one cylinder and 1 1/2 horsepower. Today, Evinrude Motors will be glad to sell you a high-performance outboard of more than 200 horsepower, if you think you can handle it. Many other companies build racing engines for boats, too. However, the fastest water speedsters — the unlimited hydroplanes — are powered by airplane engines.

Why can powerboats go so much faster than sailboats? It's not just the engine that makes the difference.

The two kinds of boats have different hulls. Sailboats, rowboats, ocean-going freighters, and lots of other slow-moving craft have displacement hulls. The hull is designed to stay in the water and plow through it, displacing water as it moves.

A displacement hull is rounded or deeply curved. It may have a large keel — a blade-shaped part extending downward from the center of the hull. Displacement hulls push aside, or displace, water as they move.

The water itself exerts drag on the hull. But the biggest slowing factors come from two masses of water — one at the bow (front) and one at the stern (rear) — that form as the boat moves through the water.

If you put a more powerful engine on a displacement hull boat, the craft will go faster. But only up to a point! As the boat speeds up, those draggy masses of water at the bow and stern become bigger and bigger. At last, there comes a point where the boat won't go any faster — no matter how strong the engine.

The only way to get high speed out of a boat is to lift its hull out of the water.

This principle is called planing. A planing hull lifts its bow out of the water as the boat gathers speed.

This Inboard Marathon craft clearly shows the advantage of a planing hull. Most of the boat is out of the water! The 454 Chevrolet engine drives the boat at 95 mph.

The fastest kind of planing hull has a perfectly flat bottom. However, this kind of hull is impossible to control at high speed. If a speeding flatboat tried to turn, it would flip over. If it ran on anything but glassy smooth water, it would wham up and down until the driver went flying like a jack-in-the-box.

So racing powerboats are designed with hulls that compromise between speediness and maneuverability. Engineers have come up with hundreds of different hull designs, trying to find winning combinations of curves.

Even so, racing hulls are apt to be skittish craft. Even expert drivers can flip over in rough water or during tricky maneuvers. Crash helmets, life jackets, and other safety gear are required in sanctioned powerboat races.

In North America, powerboat racing is controlled by the American Power Boat Association and the Canadian Boating Federation. For the sake of safety, these groups assign minimum weights to each class of racing boat. This prevents hot-dog drivers from attaching 300-horsepower engines to closet doors and calling the result a racing hydroplane.

This racer belongs to the Outboard Performance Craft (OPC) class. It has a "tunnel hull," one of the newest high-speed designs. It has two narrow planing surfaces with a square tunnel in between that runs the length of the boat. When a tunnel hull is on the move, only the engine's propeller and a few inches of the rear hull touch the water. Powered by a Johnson Stinger, this boat has a top speed of 100 mph.

A clutch of OPC boats race a closed course "match boat" contest. Engines and tunnel hulls are identical.

There are nine major classes in APBA/CBF racing. These are often subdivided into different classes of hulls and engines.

Inboards are the most numerous, as well as the oldest, type of racing powerboats. Inboards enclose the engine within the hull. They range from clunky-looking but speedy Cracker Boxes to graceful 7-Litre Inboards that look like aquatic rocket sleds.

The next largest class is the Stock Outboard. This is the least expensive way to powerboat race. You buy a runabout or hydroplane hull, attach a hot outboard engine, and go. Stockers are permitted certain modifications — and in practice,

most of the engines are a far cry from what you would buy at your local marine dealer.

Outboard Performance Craft (OPC) are more likely to resemble the family speedboat, and for this reason they are very popular with fans. They compete on many different kinds of courses and attract top drivers. Outboard and Modified Outboard boats are the aristocrats of the external engine boats. They may use exotic fuels and strange designs to achieve the fastest speeds of all outboard-style boats.

Drag boats, like their wheeled counterparts, use automobile engines to achieve fantastic speeds in a short sprint. They go the quarter-mile course at speeds up to 200 miles per hour.

Cruiser and Offshore classes involve races in open water — on the ocean, on large lakes, or on large rivers. The most glamorous of the Offshore races take place in the sea around Florida, the Bahamas, and California.

In the sport of off shore racing the boats are very expensive, and the costs of traveling from race to race are high. If you aspire to the National Championship, you'd better have at least $250,000 to play with!

And what do you get for your money? A very rough boat ride!

Offshore racing waters are rarely smooth or merely choppy. Ocean-going speedsters must be ready for waves, high winds, and storms. The boats have deep-vee bottoms that can maintain speed in rough water. The hulls are non-planing — but the craft bound out of the water in a spectacular way when they smack into high waves.

Offshore drivers take a fearful pounding during the average race. Some people who race more conventional boats claim that the Offshore guys are gluttons for punishment. But despite its discomfort, Offshore racing is really safer than most other powerboat contests.

Classic races include the Miami-Nassau dash and the Key West race. There are classes for both inboard and outboard boats, and divisions for small craft as well as large.

A swell lofts "Dante's Inferno," a Class V Inboard Offshore racer. It has a 36-foot Cigarette hull and is powered by twin MerCruiser engines. This boat can achieve a top speed of 85 mph.

The most spectacular, fastest racing boats in the world belong to the Unlimited Hydroplane class. There are no divisions. Anything goes — as long as it is a big, bad boat.

An Unlimited is a cross between a boat and an aircraft. It is powered by an aircraft engine — most often a 12-cylinder fighter-plane power-plant left over from World War II. Engines from old Spitfires, P-38's and P-51's are expensively rebuilt and modified to push the hydroplanes through the water at speeds up to 200 miles per hour.

No wonder people call them Thunderboats!

As far as hull design goes, only the designer's imagination, a 28-foot minimum length, and a 4,000 pound minimum weight restrict that "unlimited" name. "Miss Madison," on the opposite page, has a classic pointy-nose design. "Pay 'N Pak" facing the title page of this book, has what is known as a picklefork design.

Unlimited Hydroplanes compete in a circuit of 10 races each year. These include the APBA's Gold Cup Challenge, and the Gar Wood Trophy Race. The latter is named after the immortal Off-shore and Unlimited driver, who won the Gold Cup five times.

"Miss Madison" had a top speed of 175 mph in the Gold Cup Regatta held in Seattle.

Hydrofoils will comprise a new racing class in the APBA. These remarkable new craft rise out of the water on stilt-like foils. The hull thus displaces no water at all and speed potential is enormous. This 16.5-footer uses a 350 cubic inch Chevy engine, travels over 60 mph.

Canoe racers in the annual Portland Rose Festival Race use a low fiberglass craft with spray covers as they speed down Oregon's Clackamas River.

Some of the most dedicated racers of all use the simplest, most reliable power source: human muscles.

Rowing (with one oar) and sculling (with two oars) are very old sports now practiced mostly in colleges. There is an Olympic rowing competition and also a World Championship Competition for both men's and women's racing sculls.

Far more popular than the slender sculls are canoes, kayaks, and inflatable craft. These, too, are used in racing.

Olympic-type races for canoes and kayaks take place on the flat water of lakes or ponds. This kind of racing may involve one to four paddlers. It is a test of endurance and strength.

Whitewater racing on fast-flowing rivers presents a different, more exciting challenge. Besides paddling as fast as possible, the contestants must negotiate such hazards as rapids, whirlpools, and dangerous rocks.

Downriver races are timed events. One boat sets off at a time, and the one with the shortest elapsed time wins.

This kayak racer looks like he may be going down for the last time. But the danger is mostly illusion. The paddler fits in his boat like a cork in a bottle. He is virtually unsinkable in the roughest water — but he may be grateful for the crash helmet before he comes up for air!

Paddling was originally a rather lonely pastime. Hunters, fishermen, and back-country travelers used canoes, kayaks, and rafts to carry equipment. But the back-to-nature movement has attracted thousands of new paddlers who want to compete as well as travel on the water silently.

They have many events to choose from besides the classic downriver dashes. There is a canoe-sailing championship and a canoe-poling championship. There are relays and marathon events. And there is the slalom, ultimate test of a paddler's control of the boat.

Rubber raft racing is a new sport that is popular on rough, rocky rivers or small streams that may be too narrow or too shallow for canoes or kayaks.

Hundreds of crazy little boats set out on the annual World Championship Bathtub Race at Nanaimo, British Columbia.

Water slalom courses are set up in the midst of rapids or other fast-moving wildwater. There are many different obstacles that must be skillfully passed; poles that must be completely circled to the left or the right; gates made of two poles which the paddler must guide his craft between — either with or against the current; reverse gates that must be negotiated backwards; poles set up in swift eddies that must be passed in a tight turn.

Touching a pole with body, paddle, or boat costs points. So does missing a gate. In a slalom, control is far more important than mere speed or strength.

53883

For some sports fans, racing on the water is a serious business. Boat owners invest millions of dollars in hopes of winning the America's Cup or a hydroplane championship. Professional drivers earn a living in their awesome craft as they strain for higher and higher speeds.

But for most people, boat racing is simply a great way of having fun. Prizes don't mean much. Getting out on the water is the real kick. If you lose the race — or if you get dunked or "hosed down" — that's all part of the game.

Many cities and towns sponsor crazy boat races, in which people compete in just about anything that will float. You may see home-made rafts, innertubes, air mattresses, even boxes racing in the water.

The most famous of the weird races is the annual World Championship Bathtub Race, held on the third Sunday in July at Nanaimo, B.C. Hundreds of odd boats, including genuine bathtubs with outboard motors, race from Nanaimo to the city of Vancouver across the Strait of Georgia.

Go to a boat race. Take part in a boat race! Winning is the least of the fun.

Oddball boats add to the fun in the Johnson Creek Raft Race, held each spring at Milwaukie, Oregon.